FOR

I THINK YOU'D ENJOY THIS BOOK BECAUSE

FROM

PRINCIPLES FOR THE NEXT CENTURY OF WORK

Sense & Respond Press publishes short, beautiful, actionable books on topics related to innovation, digital transformation, product management, and design. Our readers are smart, busy, practical innovators. Our authors are experts working in the fields they write about.

The goal of every book in our series is to solve a real-world problem for our readers. Whether that be understanding a complex and emerging topic, or something as concrete (and difficult) as hiring innovation leaders, our books help working professionals get better at their jobs, quickly.

Jeff Gothelf & Josh Seiden

Series co-editors **Jeff Gothelf** and **Josh Seiden** wrote *Lean UX* (O'Reilly) and *Sense & Respond* (Harvard Business Review Press) together. They were co-founding principals of Neo Innovation (sold to Pivotal Labs) in New York City and helped build it into one of the most recognized brands in modern product strategy, development, and design. In 2017 they were short-listed for the Thinkers50 award for their contributions to innovation leadership. Learn more about Jeff and Josh at www.jeffgothelf.com and www.joshseiden.com.

HIRE WOMEN

Issued in print and electronic formats.
ISBN 978-0-9994769-7-0 (paperback).
ISBN 978-0-9994769-6-3 (epub).

Editor: Victoria Olsen
Designer: Mimi O Chun
Interior typesetting: Jennifer Blais
Author photograph: Darrin Estep of Darrin Estep Photography

Published in the United States by Sense & Respond Press
www.senseandrespondpress.com

Printed and bound in the United States.
1 2 3 4   20 19 18 17

Debbie Madden

HIRE WOMEN

An Agile framework for hiring and
retaining women in technology

SENSE &
RESPOND
PRESS

INTRODUCTION: WE'RE DOING IT WRONG

It was a Tuesday morning I'll never forget. I was reading through the day's emails. One from my boss was titled "compensation review." She had sent my team's compensation along to me as she had every quarter. It was data I had seen many times before. I managed 66 employees in a company of about 2,000.

I opened the spreadsheet as I had done so many times in the past. Yet on this day, I was staring at the compensation for the entire company! Somehow, I had been sent the wrong file.

I tried not to look. Honest.

But I couldn't help it. What would you have done?

I was a director at the time. I had about thirty "peers"— meaning, there were about thirty other directors at the company. I was one of two women directors. You won't be shocked to learn that I discovered I was being paid 30% less than the lowest-paid male.

I had to know: was this a blatant sexism issue, or was it a performance issue? I went to HR to inquire. After all, if I was the lowest performing director, I wanted feedback so that I could improve. As luck would have it, HR was able to compare performance of all thirty directors across multiple factors. Their conclusion was that I was being paid unfairly.

This was the 1990s and people weren't talking about equal pay with the gusto we do today. It was still taboo.

Nonetheless, I couldn't stay quiet. I raised the issue up the flagpole. After a series of aggravating conversations, I convinced the execs to match my comp to the men's.

Even though I achieved equal pay, the whole experience left a bad taste in my mouth. What if I had never seen that compensation spreadsheet? What if I hadn't had the guts to confront the execs? Despite the fact that I received a bump, I felt taken advantage of, and I can tell you that I quit that job shortly thereafter.

Fast forward almost twenty years later and I head my own company, Stride Consulting. Today, we talk about diversity and inclusion, and we talk about hiring and retaining women more than we used to.

But, despite our best intentions, we're still doing it wrong.

Hiring and retaining women doesn't start with recruiting.

Let me say that again. Hiring and retaining women doesn't start with recruiting.

Hiring women starts with ensuring every workplace is safe and inclusive for all. It starts with equal pay and zero tolerance for harassment: the foundation upon which everything else is built. On top of this foundation we must overlay an iterative process of discovering and removing bias. Then, and only then, will we truly improve hiring and retention of women. The good news? This process is achievable for teams of all sizes. And I'm going to show you how it's done.

After decades of trying dozens of different strategies and tactics, I've landed on an iterative process that works. Using the process I'm about to share with you, **Stride increased the number of women in the company by 267% in ten months!** In addition, turnover on our team was 72% lower than industry average and net profit was 47% higher.

Our agile, iterative approach to hiring and retaining women in technology is the result of years of continuous iteration and mountains of learning from failure. In fact, I'm embarrassed to say that many of the tactics I share in this book were ones that I personally messed up for years.

Now, after decades of trial and error, I'm sharing the secrets of our success with you.

But be warned, this isn't a book about being perfect and the process won't be easy. It's a book about real tactics that teams of all sizes can use. Yvette Pasqua, CTO at Meetup, said it best: "We need to acknowledge upfront that it's extra work. In order to hire and retain women and people of other underrepresented groups in tech, we have to put in the extra effort. There's simply no way around this fact."

Read on to discover how to hire and retain women on your team.

CASE STUDY: STACK OVERFLOW

Stack Overflow thought they were doing the right thing. They prioritized hiring women. In fact, it was one of the earliest decisions the founders made. But they didn't prioritize it above all else and they got into trouble. "Like all companies, Stack Overflow has an infinite list of things to do, but limited resources. In recent years, diversity and inclusion efforts have consistently been 'fairly important,' like... roughly #3 on our list of priorities—which meant they got allocated roughly zero resources," admits Jay Hanlon, EVP of Culture and Experience at Stack Overflow. With today's demand on leadership teams being spread thin in many cases, it's unfortunately all too common to see good intentions like this fail because they weren't given the true prioritization needed. Fortunately, Stack Overflow isn't willing to sit idly by. Hanlon and the team are on a mission to make a meaningful, impactful change. It's going to take time, and persistence, yet the outcomes will be worth the effort.

THE COMPETITIVE ADVANTAGE OF DIVERSE TEAMS

If you believe that hiring and retaining women in tech isn't important, then feel free to stop reading here.

If you're still reading, you'll be happy to know that diverse teams are a true competitive advantage for a company. And while this book focuses on gender diversity, the competitive advantages of diversity are true regardless of the nature of that diversity, including both acquired diversity like upbringing or work experience, as well as demographic diversity including gender, race, age, and more. The reason that diverse teams are smarter than homogeneous teams is because they make fewer subconscious assumptions that the person sitting next to them thinks like they do. If you look like me, I assume that you think like me, and then I ask you fewer questions. If you look different than me, I assume you think different than me, and then not only do I ask more questions, but you and I both ultimately pay more attention to each other. And that, in turn, makes us smarter.

If that hasn't convinced you, studies have shown that replacing an employee costs 90%–200% of the employee's annual income. So, to keep the math simple, if a tech employee earns an income of $100,000, it'll cost you $90,000 to $200,000 each time you lose an employee! So, if you think keeping turnover low isn't important, think again.

THE GENDER OPPORTUNITY

So, we've established that diverse teams are a real advantage. But, are there women out there to hire?

Yes.

Women outnumber men in the U.S. population (according to the 2017 U.S. Census Bureau) and on college campuses (according to the Federal Department of Education). Yet they hold fewer than 20% of tech jobs at big tech companies (Apple, Google, Microsoft, Facebook, and Twitter) and only 25% of tech jobs overall. And, according to *The Robert Half 2018 Salary Guide*, which surveyed 8,000 U.S. technology professionals, demand for tech hiring is expected to outpace supply for years to come.

So, there's a real gender opportunity here. In its most simple form, it boils down to this: tech demand is greater than supply. And the supply of women is greater than what is being used. Right now, the world's population is 50% women yet we are using only 25% of them. Therefore, our job is to find the missing 25% of women.

That's right. Each of our tech teams could be 25% bigger when we figure out how to hire and retain more women!

Yeah, yeah, I know what you are going to say: "that's oversimplifying the problem." or "that doesn't even make sense. It's not like there's a pool of women technologists lining up at our doors waiting to be hired. These women don't in fact exist. If they did exist, they'd be applying for the jobs."

I respectfully disagree.

Women technologist are out there. It's our job to find them, hire them, and retain them. It's my quest to teach you how.

Note: I'd like to take a moment to recognize that there are many individuals who do not identify as female or male, and whose gender identity exists outside the binary options of woman or man. It feels wrong to say that I am using the word 'woman' to encompass all individuals who do not identify as male. It also feels wrong to avoid gender altogether in this book about diversity. But I can't list all gender options in each sentence that references gender. So I will use 'woman' or 'female' as I write, and in doing so will be referring to all individuals who refer to themselves as female. I welcome input on how to improve upon this for future books and blogs.

CHAPTER 1: PLAY FAIR WITH EQUAL PAY

Like I said earlier, hiring women doesn't start with recruiting. I can't tell you how many times someone has gotten excited about a big diversity initiative and they start by spending hours of time sourcing women developers on LinkedIn.

Nope. Wrong.

Hiring women starts with turning your workplace into a fair and inclusive environment. It starts with equal pay and zero tolerance of harassment. These two elements are the foundation of true diversity and inclusion. They are the center, the core. Once these two elements are in place, retention is next. Then and only then can you focus on hiring more women.

When I say this, people don't believe that equal pay and zero tolerance for harassment are possible to achieve. I can tell you with certainty that they are. This chapter and the next go into detail on how to achieve both. You can tackle one at a time, or work on both in parallel.

Creating equal pay isn't easy. It requires commitment to a system that evaluates each individual relative to their peers and, at the same time, enables fluidity within the system. Yet it is possible.

To me, equal pay means paying two people who are doing the same job, at the same performance level, equally. My barometer for success is: if the salary data for my entire company were to wind up on the front page of *The New York Times* by accident, every employee at the company would understand and agree with everyone else's salary. Notice, I'm not advocating for an open book policy. Employee salaries are confidential and an employee has a right to keep that information confidential. What I'm advocating for is a fair system that would hold up if fully discovered.

Paying people equally for equal work doesn't mean we wave a magic wand and make all salaries identical. You wouldn't pay a junior developer and a CTO the same amount, regardless of which role was held by a woman and which by a man. Rather, it means we clearly define each role on the team, and create a clear path to promotion. Think of these next steps as your Equal Pay Road Map.

STEP 1: CREATE SKILL CATEGORIES

A **skill category** is a broad skill that you expect a group of individuals on a team to have. For example: Internal Leadership. A skill category should to be broad enough that it can be improved on over several years. For an engineering team, skill categories might include:

» Agile Engineering Practices
» Technical Skills
» Domain Knowledge
» Internal Leadership

Once you have a handful of skill categories, define beginner, intermediate, and advanced level expectations for each skill category. For example:

Skill Category #1: Agile Engineering Practices

Level: Beginner

» Demonstrates awareness of, and interest in, Agile Engineering principles
» Is able to be an effective pair, both driving and navigating
» Is open to feedback and gives effective feedback to developers

» Is learning Test-Driven Development (TDD) and estimation

Level: Intermediate
» Practices multiple Agile Engineering practices, including TDD, Pair Programming, and Iteration Planning
» Teaches others Agile Engineering practices
» Understands the value of agile ceremonies and can teach others how to facilitate them

Level: Advanced
» Understands the benefits and pitfalls of Lean, Scrum, and Kanban
» Teaches fellow developers how to introduce Agile Engineering practices
» Can teach skeptical co-workers TDD, Pairing, Estimation

You can have an "Expert" level as well. More than four levels starts to get complex. Find the number of levels that works for your organization.

STEP 2: DEVELOP A CAREER LADDER AND ROLE MATRIX

Once you have your skill categories fleshed out, create a **career ladder** to give employees a clear path to promotion. A sample engineering team career ladder might be:

1. Junior Developer
2. Mid-level Developer
3. Senior Developer
4. Lead Developer

5. Engineering Manager
6. Director, Engineering
7. VP, Engineering
8. CTO

Each rung on the ladder is a role on your team.

Then, overlay your skill categories onto your career ladder to get your **role matrix**. In essence, this creates the set of skills required to be eligible for promotion to the next level. For example, if you overlay the first four rungs on the career ladder above with the four skill categories above you get:

Role Matrix

Junior Developer
» Requires at least Beginner level in all four skill categories

Mid-level Developer
» Requires Intermediate level in
Agile Engineering Practices
» Requires Intermediate level in at least one other
skill category

Senior Developer
» Requires Intermediate level in all four skill categories
» Requires Advanced level in at least one other
skill category

Lead Developer
» Requires Intermediate level in all four skill
categories
» Requires Advanced level in Agile Engineering
practices and one other skill category

STEP 3: ESTABLISH SALARY BANDS

Now we must align compensation with the role matrix: every role on the career ladder gets a **salary band** assigned to it. For example, all Junior Developer salaries fall within one distinct salary band. Ideally, salary bands are narrow. Roughly a $15,000–$25,000 difference should separate the bottom from the top of each salary band. Some teams overlap bands, and some do not. For example, you can have Junior Developer salary overlap Mid-level Developer salary, or you can keep the bands distinct.

Congratulations! You now have a clear definition of the skills required for each role, and the salary attached to each. I strongly recommend you share your Skill Categories, Career Ladder, Role Matrix, and Salary Bands with your entire team. We even share ours with recruiting candidates who make it to the final stage.

PROTIP: ALLOW FOR PROMOTIONS AT ANY TIME.

Whenever a manager, employee or anyone else in the company believes an individual has achieved the required levels, the employee is nominated for a promotion, whether that takes six months or six years. The process for nomination, review, approval and announcement should be created and shared with the entire company.

STEP 4: BUMP-UP PAY

This is the catch-all step. It's the step that ensures we remain competitive. Sometimes, no matter how fair we are inside our company, the outside world leaps ahead. Fair market value of employees fluctuates constantly. I don't advise adjusting internal salaries up or down frequently. But an annual review of how your salaries compare to market rates is a good idea.

For employees who fall behind market pay, proactively offer **bump-up pay**. For example, if a developer is earning $105,000 and you find that new hires who are on par with her are getting offered $110,000 to join your team, then the developer earning $105,000 should get a $5,000 off-cycle bump in pay. This should happen proactively, without the employee having to ask for it. Depending on the size of your organization, the responsibility for monitoring this may fall to either HR or your leadership team.

CASE STUDY: STRIDE CONSULTING

At Stride Consulting, we abide by this process. Yet that doesn't mean it's one and done. In the past four years, we've revamped these steps three times, which equates to roughly every time the team has doubled in size. And our salary bands are refreshed once a year. We hire a third-party salary data firm, share with them all current job roles, and plot out where we fall relative to the market. Abiding by these steps is an ongoing commitment to taking an honest look at the needs of the team and then ensuring you are doing all you can to assess each employee fairly.

HOW TRANSPARENT SHOULD YOU BE?

You might be wondering how transparent you ought to be about salary. The process I've seen work best is to be 100% transparent with the salary bands. Show every employee the full salary ladder. And then keep the individual salaries confidential. Every employee should sign an offer letter with their employer that contains the conditions of their employment. Compensation is one piece of the agreement, and yet there are many other factors. Every employee deserves privacy when it comes to personal data, and keeping employee salary confidential between the individual and their manager is best.

You saw what happened to me. I wound up seeing compensation for my entire company, and it was unfair. Instead, make salary bands internally transparent and ensure everyone is in the right band. If your entire salary ledger were to wind up in the wrong hands know that you could look that person in the eye and justify every number on the page.

A NOTE ON FAIRNESS INSIDE EACH SALARY BAND

It is true that there will be some wiggle room inside each of the bands. The alternative, which is setting precise salaries for each and every minor movement along the ladder and leaving no room for someone to prove they are worth more, is quite demotivating, and will likely result in star performers feeling undervalued and quitting.

Ten years ago, I was running a team of forty software engineers. We had salary bands, yet the team asked for more transparency. We responded by creating precise salaries for every step on the ladder, and precise durations at each level. So, for example, everyone had to be a Junior Developer for two years before becoming a Mid-level Developer. The year after we made this change, turnover skyrocketed. And it was the highest performers who were leaving. When we spoke with them at their exit interviews, they each told a similar tale: all of the motivation to hustle was sucked out of them. They knew that no matter how well they did, their fate was sealed. They knew exactly how much money they'd make far out into the future, and that was unfulfilling for them. For me, it was a lesson learned the hard way.

So, there needs to be some wiggle room inside bands, but not too much. And the manager must be held accountable for fairness inside each band. To ensure that happens, you can analyze salary inside each band by gender and if any biases are identified you can address them.

On a related note, New York State recently banned employers from asking what a candidate's current or past salary is for the sole reason that this put women at a disadvantage. We are not legally allowed to ask candidates what their current or past compensation was. So it's up to us to vet candidates and correctly place them at the appropriate level inside the organization.

If someone knocks the interview out of the park, and wants $20,000 more than you believe they deserve, give them a fair offer and tell them the truth. I often say, "every offer I make has to be fair. If a developer who's worked here for three years discovers what I offered you to join the team, they have to understand that number."

PROTIP: NEVER EVER EVER EVER GET FOOLED INTO PAYING OVER MARKET FOR A NEW HIRE.

The minute you offer a new hire a salary that will anger one of your current employees is the minute you've put your culture at risk.

CHAPTER 2: STAY SAFE WITH ZERO TOLERANCE OF HARASSMENT

Equally foundational as equal pay is zero tolerance of harassment. Harassment in the workplace is a sensitive topic and must be taken seriously at all times. I firmly believe this is table stakes. If you want an inclusive work environment that women and all others want to be part of, it must start with safety for every single individual. Here's how:

STEP 1: DEFINE YOUR TERMS AND MAINTAIN A CODE OF CONDUCT

There's a good chance your company already has a code of conduct and a definition of harassment, so take a look at them before re-creating the wheel. Harassment can come in all shapes and sizes, so defining your terms is only the beginning. In order to truly have a safe, inclusive environment for all, you must seek to continuously enable everyone to be heard.

Your company should not tolerate subtle or blatant racism, sexism, homophobia, transphobia, harassment, or other kinds of bias. That should include micro-aggressions, or what we at Stride call "**subtle-isms**." Subtle-isms are small things that make others feel uncomfortable, things that we all sometimes do by mistake. For example, saying "it's so easy my grandmother could do it" is a subtle-ism. Or telling a joke about a class of people. Like the other social rules, this one is sometimes accidentally broken. If it happens by accident, apologize and move on.

Include your definitions and code of conduct in an employee handbook and as part of your employee onboarding process have all new hires sign an acknowledgement form, saying they've read the handbook, know what's in it, and are aware that updates will be made from time to time. All employees are accountable for knowing where the employee handbook is and being familiar with its contents.

Have your HR manager or equivalent email the entire company every time a handbook item is updated.

PRO TIP: PUT YOUR HARASSMENT DEFINITION AND YOUR CODE OF CONDUCT INTO AN EMPLOYEE HANDBOOK, BUT DO NOT PRINT IT.

Embrace agility and make it a dynamic document that changes over time. Use Google docs or another online tool to store your handbook. Keep a tight leash on who has editing access to your digital handbook. The last thing you want is someone updating it without everyone knowing.

CASE STUDY: *THE NEW YORK TIMES*

Nick Rockwell, the CTO at *The New York Times*, makes inclusion and a safe workplace a top priority. "We solicit as much feedback as possible on all of our policy or culture-related initiatives. One way we do this is by opening them to the whole technology organization through shared Google docs, where we encourage ideas, feedback, and suggestions via comments," notes Rockwell. "We use this feedback to continually iterate and improve our policies."

In fact, the technology department at the *Times* also has two dedicated resource groups, Women in Technology and Diversity in Digital, that are devoted to identifying issues, offering feedback and developing initiatives in order to improve their diversity and inclusion efforts. For example, the Women in Technology group put together a list of microaggressions members had experienced, so everyone would know how to identify and address them.

STEP 2: THE HANDSHAKE DEAL

As a leader, it's your job to make a visible and specific commitment to enforcing your code of conduct and its values—and ensuring that everyone else does too. Do this by discussing culture with candidates at every job offer. Share that your company has a zero tolerance policy on harassment and take a minute to detail what that means. I go so far as to tell candidates that if they don't believe in our code of conduct and our core values, they should turn down the job offer.

Then I actually take this one step further. Every single time I give a job offer, I include a "Handshake Deal." The handshake deal is an unwritten, verbal agreement between me and the employee. It articulates what we expect of each other.

I believe that most job offers fail to discuss protocol for having difficult conversations between employee and employer once the employee starts work. The result is that employees don't feel comfortable sharing when they are unhappy. This leads to employees mentally checking out long before they actually leave a job. Employees learn to keep their opinions to themselves and show up to work with a lackadaisical attitude, which can dampen the morale of those around them.

To combat this problem, every job offer must include an honest, two-way conversation up front about each person's role in the employee's ongoing happiness at work. Here's a sample script I use:

> Your end of the handshake, what I expect of you should you choose to come work on our team, is that you own advocating for you.
>
> As we work together, we'll get to know each other. I aim to get to know you as a person, know what makes you happy, frustrated, and energized. But I don't have a crystal ball. I'm never going to know you as well as you know you. So, it's up to you to advocate for you. If there comes a time when you need something from me that you aren't getting, you need to raise your hand and tell someone. If no one knows what's on your mind, we can't help you.
>
> My end of this deal, what I ask that you expect from me, is that I come to work each day and aim to do right by you: to create a safe place for you to work, to treat you with respect, and to listen when you come to me with questions, concerns, and feedback. I should lead

through doing and be willing to do anything myself that I ask of you.

And we both must expect of each other that we understand life isn't a fairytale. We can't sprinkle pixie dust on a problem and make it magically disappear. We are running a business and things sometimes take time to resolve. So, once you raise your hand and advocate for you, you become part of the problem-solving team with me.

If you can't shake on this, I am asking you to turn down this job offer. If you do shake on this, and there comes a time when you can no longer uphold your end of the deal, I ask that you let me know so we can either figure out a way to get you back to a place where you can uphold your end of the deal, or we can talk about transitioning you out of the company.

STEP 3: TAKE ALL ACCUSATIONS SERIOUSLY

Hopefully, you will never have to deal with an employee accusing someone of harassing them. However, it does happen. If it does :

» Share the details with your HR department and lawyer immediately.
» Stick to the facts. Now's not the time for interpretation, opinion, exaggeration, or generalization.
» Document everything and ensure everything is kept confidential.
» Do not go directly to the accused party before you speak with your lawyer.
» Your lawyer is the the one to guide you on how to proceed.

A zero tolerance policy on harassment does NOT mean that you are creating a finger-pointing environment. If someone is accused of harassment, the company and its leadership are accountable for investigating and completing a due diligence process to get to the root of the issue from all sides. This book isn't about due diligence, and I'm not a lawyer, so I'll sum up by saying that it's critically important to work alongside HR and a lawyer whenever you are dealing with a harassment issue in your workplace. And, if you believe the HR department or your lawyer are not handling the issue appropriately, it's a good idea to get a second professional opinion.

A note to all of the tech leads, managers, Directors and VPs reading this: if you are a manager, you are liable. It's not only the CEO and executive team who are accountable. If you are a team lead, or in any position of authority or leadership inside a company, you are accountable and liable for any harassment or wrongdoing. It's not okay to wait for someone else to take action. If you are on a team and learn about harassment of any kind, tell someone on your legal or HR team. If you have questions regarding the details of your liability, speak with your company's legal team.

PRO TIP: IT IS CRITICALLY IMPORTANT TO HAVE YOUR HR DEPARTMENT AND LAWYER REVIEW AND APPROVE YOUR DEFINITION OF HARASSMENT, YOUR CODE OF CONDUCT, AND ANY OTHER ARTIFACTS REGARDING HARASSMENT THAT YOUR COMPANY SANCTIONS. If you don't have a professional on staff who can approve these definitions, email me; I will give you the name of our lawyer.

A NOTE ON MANDATORY DIVERSITY TRAINING

People hate being told what to do. It seems like an obvious statement, yet too often companies drive culture initiatives from the top down.

Think about it. Imagine you're sitting at your desk, and you get an email from your boss that reads, "we're not doing a great job at diversity hiring and retention, so we've brought in a diversity expert to tell us how to get better. Everyone is required to attend the training Monday at 9am." This seems innocent enough but be honest, aren't you thinking "I'm not biased. Sure, I'll attend the training, but it doesn't apply to me. I'm a good person. I'm sure I'm already doing all I can."

That's what happens. People dig in their heels and resist learning, even though we mean well. In "Why Diversity Fails," Frank Dobbin, professor of sociology at Harvard University, and Alexandra Kalev, professor of sociology at Tel Aviv University, argue that's because "people rebel against rules that threaten their autonomy." Yet, despite this fact, a full 100% of Fortune 500 companies hold mandatory diversity training programs.

Let's all agree to stop the insanity and end these programs. They are top down, talk at you, and reprimanding.

(I've just said to stop mandatory training, but New York State is now requiring mandatory training. Ugh!)

CHAPTER 3: DISCOVER BIAS

Congratulations. You've addressed the foundational core of hiring and retention. You've worked on equal pay and zero tolerance of harassment. I recognize that implementing these changes and shifting company culture takes time. In some cases of enterprise teams, it might take a lot of time. Stick with it and keep impacting change. Now let's move on to the process of discovering and removing bias.

Take another look at our hiring and retention circle:

Equal pay and zero harassment are at the core. Once these foundational elements are in place, your next job is to discover where bias exists inside your hiring and retention processes and then remove as much bias as possible.

Discovering bias and then removing it is the secret sauce to hiring and retaining women. Whether you currently have a lot of women on your team or none, you and your team should expect to go through several iterations of discovering and then removing bias in order to get the whole system to an efficient state. Depending on the nature of the biases, they may each be easy or difficult to find. And after you find them, determining how to prioritize them becomes the key to removing bias successfully. It truly is an iterative loop:

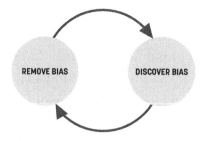

In order to discover bias, we have to understand what it is. There are three types of bias relevant to gender:

» Conscious bias, or prejudice in favor of or against something

» Unconscious bias, or quick judgments of people and situations that our brains make without us realizing

» Confirmation bias, or the tendency to interpret new evidence as confirmation of our existing beliefs or theories

Bias of all three types exist in the workplace. The hardest type to find and remove is unconscious bias, because it's invisible.

The case study about Heidi Roizen is my favorite example of unconscious gender bias. A Columbia Business School professor named Frank Flynn presented his class with a case study about a successful venture capitalist. Unbeknownst to the students, Professor Flynn gave the class two different case studies. Half of the students read about a venture capitalist named Heidi and the other half read about a venture capitalist named Howard. Other than the name change, the two case studies were identical. Yet, while students ranked Heidi and Howard equally competent, both male and female students liked Howard and disliked Heidi.

Nobody truly knows why this is. Perhaps it's because we unconsciously associate women with the home and men with a career, and when a woman challenges this unconscious bias we react with anger. We know that these types of implicit bias exist inside our brains, and many of us make associations all day long that we don't even realize we are making. If you think you're in the minority and don't have any implicit bias, I encourage you to take an Implicit Bias test (a link is included under Project Implicit in the Reading List at the end of this book).

Regardless of the reason for the bias, the best thing we can all do is accept the reality that unconscious gender bias exists—always has, always will. That means you, me, and everyone else is biased, and we don't even know it. By accepting the realities of gender bias, we can be smart about discovering where it lurks, and this gives us a better chance at outsmarting it.

FIND VOLUNTEERS

You may be asking yourself at this point: Discovering bias feels like a whole ton of work. Am I supposed to do it all by myself? Ideally, no. It's best if you can form a self-organized, autonomous team of people who are excited and passionate about volunteering to help with diversity and inclusion initiatives.

Seek out volunteers in your organization to own either pieces of your diversity and inclusion initiatives or the entire thing. We have a Diversity and Inclusion Committee, and a Mentorship Committee. Developers volunteer to be on the committee. The committees set annual goals and have the full support of the leadership team to achieve their goals.

Whether you have a committee or embrace volunteers in another way, the key to success is remembering that people hate being told what to do. The more that individuals can opt in, the better.

CASE STUDY: AMY AND ERIC, PART 1

Amy was a developer on a team of twelve people, inside a company of 105 employees. She'd been at the company for two years. She was passionate about increasing the number of women engineers on her team. So she set out to find volunteers.

After searching for two weeks, Amy couldn't find a single person to volunteer. Some folks didn't see hiring women as a top priority. Others were intrigued but had big deadlines around the corner.

At a minimum, it would be ideal to have at least one other person volunteer. But, given no one was volunteering, Amy decided to go it alone and get a quick visible win, and then ask for volunteers again. At the next company meeting, Amy presented the results of a diversity survey to the entire company, and compared the data to their industry. It turns out Amy's team was losing women at a rate three times that of the industry. Seeing the problem visually was enough to awaken the passion in one of Amy's co-workers, Eric.

She found a quick win and got one person on board. It doesn't take a village; small teams are powerful.

LISTEN TO YOUR TEAM

Now that you have a definition of bias and a team of volunteers, you can start to discover where bias exists inside your company, so that you can improve hiring and retaining women.

Discovering bias is hard. And it is an iterative process. This is not a one-and-done process; rather it's an ongoing approach to continuously improving hiring and retention. Discovering bias must start with listening and seeking to understand. It can't start with telling people what to do. As I mentioned above, people hate being told what to do.

Instead of telling people what to do, start with listening. Listen by gathering a cross section of input regarding what your team and company believe they currently do well and what they believe are your greatest areas for improvement when it comes to hiring and retaining women.

You are about to gather a lot of data from all of your listening. Be prepared to capture all of that data somewhere because we are going to need it later on. That doesn't have to be fancy: a Google doc or notepad will do.

To get people to talk with you openly and honestly, let them know that you are interested in improving gender diversity and inclusion on your team, and as the first step in this process, you want to hear their thoughts and input.

Listen to as many different groups as possible. Gather input from:

» The individuals on your team
» A cross section of employees at your company
» People in your industry and community
» Past recruiting candidates
» Customers

There are many ways to listen and gather insights. I recommend:

ONE-ON-ONES

If you already have recurring one-on-one meetings, discuss diversity and inclusion as part of the next round of meetings.

If you don't have one-on-ones as part of your culture, ask for volunteers to chat with you individually. Also talk with a handful of past recruiting candidates who recently interviewed with your team and turned you down.

I recommend asking open-ended questions during the one-on-ones, such as:

» *What do you think we do well when it comes to:*
  • Diversity and inclusion
  • Hiring women and non-binary individuals
  • Retaining women and non-binary individuals
» *What do you wish we did better when it comes to:*
  • Diversity and inclusion
  • Hiring women and non-binary individuals

- Retaining women and non-binary individuals
  » *Would you be interested in being part of a volunteer task force on diversity and inclusion?*
  » *What other input or thoughts do you have on this topic?*
  » *Are you okay with me anonymizing your feedback and sharing trends I'm hearing with the whole company?*

We'll talk more about one-on-ones in the next chapter on Removing Bias.

PRO TIP: DO NOT FORCE CONVERSATIONS OR MAKE THEM MANDATORY.
Anyone who discusses diversity and inclusion with you should do so on an opt-in, volunteer basis.

SURVEYS

In addition to having one-on-one conversations, send short, targeted surveys to your team using SurveyMonkey or a similar tool. Surveys are a great way to give everyone an equal voice.

You can choose to make the survey answers anonymous. I suggest setting up surveys so that the team understands their purpose, asking open-ended questions just like in the one-on-ones, and adding in one or two rating-scale questions. For example:

Hi team,

I've been reading about best practices in hiring and retaining women. I'm very interested in learning your thoughts regarding how we currently handle diversity and inclusion at Acme Co. If you have three minutes, I'd appreciate you answering this short, optional survey. Note: answers will remain anonymous.

Question 1: On a scale of 1–10 (10 being the best) how successful do <u>you</u> feel Acme Co currently is at
  » Hiring women and non-binary individuals

» Retaining women and non-binary individuals

» Having an interview process free of gender bias

Question 2: What do you think we do well when it comes to hiring and retaining women and non-binary individuals?

Question 3: What do you wish we did better when it comes to hiring and retaining women and non-binary individuals?

RESEARCH

Research is a great complement to one-on-ones and surveys. Reading gives you a look into what a broad range of people are discussing. Don't let this book be the last thing you read on hiring women. Seek to soak up as much knowledge as possible so that you can form your own best practices. Sources of reading include:

» Glassdoor, Yelp, and other online reviews of <u>your</u> company
   • Do you know what your employees and others are saying about your company online?

» Glassdoor, Yelp, and other online reviews of <u>other</u> companies
   • Learn how you compare with other companies and teams. Learn what other companies are doing well, and what they are failing at.

» Blogs and books on the latest trends in gender diversity and inclusion.
   • *Harvard Business Review* publishes top-notch content on diversity. See the links to the articles in the Reading List at the end of this book.

» Websites of companies who have a reputation for strong diversity, such as Pandora and Etsy.

There's no "right way" to listen. The most important things are to **spend time listening** and **document your learnings**.

DESIGN A BIAS DISCOVERY MIND MAP

Take all of the data, learnings and insights you gathered from the activities detailed earlier in this book—the equal pay road map, zero tolerance of harassment process, and listening—and use it as input for this next exercise. Your goal is to literally paint a picture of where bias might lurk inside your company. I'm calling this picture a Bias Discovery Mind Map.

A Mind Map is a diagram that visually organizes information. It is centered around one core concept, with subsets of the core concept branching off of it. To craft your Bias Discovery Mind Map:

> » **Gather your volunteer team for a brainstorming session.** Ask them to come prepared to brainstorm where bias might exist, both inside your organization as well as externally (as part of your hiring process or even inside your marketing materials). Also bring with you all notes and thoughts from the listening process. You will ideally take 1-2 hours to complete the Bias Discovery Mind Map brainstorming session.
> » **Start by drawing one circle.** Write "Hiring & Retention" inside of it.
> » **Brainstorm areas of potential or known bias** inside your hiring and retention practices or inside your company (see diagram below).

As tempting as it may be, don't worry just yet about which biases you are going to try to fix. And don't worry about how you will fix them. For now, just know that you are likely to find many areas of existing or potential bias. We'll tackle prioritizing the bias in the next chapter.

In fact, during your brainstorm session, you may not even know yet if bias exists. For example, a potential area of bias is in job descriptions. But, how will you know for certain if your job descriptions are biased? As you brainstorm, you may or may not be confident in your knowledge of where bias exists in each area of your business. Not to worry. For now, just bring an open mind and think of as many *potential* areas of bias as possible.

Here's a sample **Bias Discovery Mind Map**. Every team is different and this example is far from complete. It's just meant to get you started:

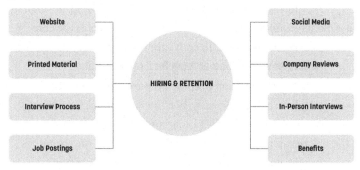

For now, don't worry about every last detail. Focus on fleshing out the Mind Map as much as possible. Drill down as many levels as needed in order to include everything that touches your hiring and retention practices on the Mind Map.

SET GOALS

After you complete your first brainstorm of your Bias Discovery Mind Map, it's common to feel overwhelmed. There's a lot to do and only 24 hours in any given day.

At this point, you haven't yet drilled into each potential area of bias, so you don't yet truly know which areas are on fire versus which areas aren't that concerning. But, before we delve into all of that, we need to set a goal. Think about what you and your team aim to achieve in the next year in terms of hiring women. What are your goals? What are you anti-goals?

Come up with one or two hiring and/or retention goals for the year. For example, an annual goal might be:

» By January 1st, increase the percentage of women developers by X%.

» By January 1st, decrease turnover of women by X%.

Come up with one or two anti-goals to ensure you don't veer so far down one path that you wind up messing up another important measure of success in your business.

Anti-goals could be:

» Don't decrease the team's average velocity.

» Don't increase the turnover of men.

If your team or company already has a goal setting system in place, like Objectives and Key Results, Rocks, or Key Performance Indicators, try to align your hiring & retention goals with these.

CASE STUDY: AMY AND ERIC, PART 2

Amy and Eric got feedback from their CEO that, even though the company was losing women at a rate three times that of the industry, nothing more was needed to improve diversity on the team. They were crushed. They wanted time away from writing code to work on this and felt a small amount of effort would go a long way. But they realized they hadn't given the CEO a specific goal they wished to achieve as a result of their efforts.

So they asked the CEO if they could take one hour a week for six months to work on diversity initiatives. They set a goal of doubling the number of women engineers on the team at the end of that six month period.

As a result, Amy and Eric were given the green light to form a Diversity Committee and were given six months to achieve their goals.

PRIORITIZE BIAS

Now that you've got your first pass at your Bias Discovery Mind Map and your goals, it's time to figure out which areas on your Mind Map are in most need of attention. For each item on your Mind Map, have your team answer the question, "is the health of this item good, mediocre, or poor?"

This isn't an exact science. It's more important to rank each item against each other, relative to all the other items. It's very similar to t-shirt size estimating in software development. With t-shirt estimating, Agile teams label each story as small, medium, and large, based on how big they are relative to each other. The same theory applies here. If you can't choose, write a question mark.

A nice visual way to approach this is to color-code each item on your Mind Map:

» Red = poor health
» Yellow = mediocre health
» Green = good health

You could also choose to assign numbers, where Green is 3, Yellow is 2, Red is 1.

The mechanics of triaging the health of each item into Red, Yellow or Green depends on your team, and depends on the knowledge you have of each area of the business, as well as its impact on hiring women. Let's stick with job descriptions as an example of potential bias. Do you know with high certainty that your job descriptions feel stale, biased, poor? Do you know with high certainty that they were recently updated by someone on the recruiting team with knowledge of gender-neutral wording, and

11. Diversity starts w/ a safe, inclusive workplace
   - equal pay
   - zero harassment -
   - discover/remove biases

14. how to find the 25% of the pop that are women
   and would like a tech job

   formal job descs / skills / salary bands
   - fair market value annual reviews
   - bring people up to the new person
   - share all bands w/ everyone

27. Microaggressions list

31. No mandatory diversity training?
   (implicit bias) test — what instead?

36. Diversity team?   pg 40   — Gartner
   1:1, Survey, Research   2/14

42. Goals?
   Agile process

48. ideas
   blog - women in Tech   — LinkedIn
                             — Gartner

52. Better 1:1's
   Are there biases in Perf Reviews?

55. Job desc. must extend to reduce them

57. women coder groups

WFAE42413 African elephants, Amboseli National Park, Kenya © ichywong/Shutterstock.com

have seen them produce a diverse applicant pool? Or, do you have little insight into the health of your job descriptions?

Honesty is key here. The less you know about the true health of each item, and its positive or negative impact on your ability to hire women, the longer this exercise is going to take. It might not be possible to do it all in one sitting. Folks might have to go off and do some sleuthing to learn more about the details of particular areas. It's up to you how you approach the Red, Yellow, Green assignment. This is one of those iterative situations where the best path forward is to take an educated guess and be willing to come back to it later.

CREATE YOUR BACKLOG

Once you've got your Mind Map color coded into Red, Yellow, Green, the next step is creating a high-level backlog. What I find is best is a simple to-do board with three lists:

» Green items go onto the "Low Priority" backlog
» Yellow items become your "Medium Priority" backlog
» Red items become your "High Priority" backlog

At this point, you're still not describing the problem in detail. If this were a piece of software we were building, and we were creating a proper team backlog, we might create epics or stories or maybe even tasks. Some teams would want to estimate how long each item would take to address. That level of detail isn't required yet.

Once you have your Red, Yellow and Green backlog, take a look at it. Is everything on fire? Is everything Red? Or are there some things in Green and Yellow? Feel free to take the Red, Yellow, and Green items and use any prioritization or backlog tool or technique to organize it. Remember, this isn't an exact science either. If you colored an item Yellow but it will take two minutes to make it Green, then maybe it's worth doing sooner rather than later.

The more you can mirror an Agile team the better. I strongly suggest getting into a regular scrum cadence. Have someone take on the Product Owner role, defined by Agile Alliance as the person responsible for "managing the product backlog in order to achieve the desired outcome that a product development team seeks to accomplish."

CHAPTER 4: REMOVE BIAS

Once you have a high-priority backlog, take a good look at it. Your job now is to figure out how to spend your time—and on which items—to remove bias in a way that aligns with the goal you've defined.

Even with a high priority backlog and an annual goal, you might not have clarity on how broken some items truly are. You might not have clarity on what to work on first. You also might not have a handle on exactly how many hours or days it will take to fix something, and what the impact of that fix will be. Here are a few tips to guide you:

> » Consult Douglas Hubbard's *How to Measure Anything*. This is the best book I've ever read on how to measure things that you'd otherwise think are immeasurable. It's worth a read.
> » If you feel like something is broken, it probably is. It's worth prioritizing it and then digging into the details to learn if it's truly in need of attention. What's most important is starting *somewhere* and doing *something*.

WHAT WORKS FOR RETENTION?

If the road ahead of you looks daunting, know that removing bias in your organization goes a long way in improving both hiring and retention of women. Not only will this work help you hire for diversity, it will help you retain your hires, and that will be beneficial for your team.

What follows are some of the best tips, tricks and tactics that I've seen work in removing bias and enabling the hiring of more women on teams big and small. Feel free to pick and choose from these tactics, or from others that aren't mentioned here, to find the ones that work best for your team and that align with the areas you have decided to focus on. I'll happily compare notes and talk about ideas that aren't on this page. Reach out to me and if you want to talk about different tactics.

Also, as you read through these tactics, reference your Mind Map. Maybe you thought an area of your hiring process was in good shape, but after you read an idea below you might reconsider. Embrace change and shuffle around your priority list in your scrums as needed.

I'm not going to go into detail on the obvious stuff, the stuff you've likely heard before and may or may not already be doing. I'll bullet point them below.

» **Check your website language and images.** Make sure the pictures on your site aren't all white dudes playing foosball. Say somewhere on your careers page that you are committed to diversity and inclusion. Focusing on diversity and inclusion doesn't mean you have to use only feminine imagery and language. Pandora's career page simply states "Diversity at Pandora: Pandora is committed to playing a role in creating a more equitable society in which our business, employees, and communities will thrive."

» **Offer benefits for a diverse group of employees.** Offer as generous a family leave policy as you can afford. Talk about different types of benefits and events that will appeal to different demographics.

» **Support groups that support diversity.** There are many organizations, both for profit and not-for-profit ones, that support diversity in tech. There are organizations that focus on every aspect of diversity. Support these organizations in any way you can. You can support them by: providing space for their events, volunteering to mentor their members, donating money, coaching their members on a life skill like how to interview and get a job, etc.

» **Minimize the number of requirements listed in job descriptions.** Women will apply to a job if they believe they meet 100% of the job requirements, whereas

men will apply if they believe they meet 60% of
the job requirements. So avoid the temptation to
overstuff the job requirements list on job postings.

Now let's look at some of the more nuanced and less obvious
tactics that should be part of your ongoing culture management:

RAISE YOUR VOICE

It's interesting to me how often I hear people say "there's no reason
I should write a blog on women in tech, I don't have anything new
to say."

Here's the thing. That's not the point. The reason you
should write a blog about women in tech is so that people who
don't know you can know your opinion. And then, when those
people are seeking their next job, some of them will think "hey,
I don't personally know this person, but what this person writes
really resonates with me, I think I might like working with this
person." And then, some of those people will apply to work at your
company.

If you have a public opinion that advocates for diversity and
inclusion on tech teams, whether you write a blog, give a talk, or
record a podcast, then the community will know where you stand.

There are two ways to have a public opinion that others
notice:

1. Talk about a topic and hope that others will find it
   interesting.
2. Talk about a topic that is already trending and ride
   the wave of that topic.

Both ways are important. The second way is more likely to
get heard by a wider audience because people are already talking
about it and seeking it out.

On March 1, 2017, the *New York Times* published an article called "Uber Case Could Be a Watershed for Women in Tech." The article stated, "if Uber mounted an honest investigation into its culture and pledged to transparently remake what ails it, it could become a model for the [tech] industry."

A model? Were they kidding? I think my body temperature rose 10 degrees in thirty seconds. I was pissed. I pulled out my laptop and wrote a passionate rebuttal to said *New York Times* article, and posted it on Medium and LinkedIn (you can find it on the Reading List at the end of the book). Within 24 hours, my blog was the #1 recommended article on all of Medium, and within 48 hours, CNBC had asked me to write a follow-up piece.

I'm quite sure this blog wasn't the most profound piece I've ever written. I'm even quite sure there are still grammatical errors in it to this day. Yet I was in the right place at the right time. I had a public opinion on a trending topic: people were *desperately* seeking content on Uber's culture. Within one month of writing that blog post, seven female developers applied to work on our team and credited this blog as the reason for applying. Months and even years later, women developers are still mentioning that piece as the reason for applying to work with us. That blog post was part of an aligned strategy for our diversity initiative. Diversity means something to me and I took a stand behind it publicly.

There are a slew of articles and blogs that I've written over the years in which I share my opinions on diversity and inclusion. Some I write out of passion, some I write because I disagree with something else I've read, some I write because someone asks me to elaborate on a thought I have. If I can get a couple of articles a year that garner some level of attention for topics I care passionately about, it's a win.

The thing that stops most of us from writing a compelling article that gets noticed is that most of us don't write enough crappy articles. We're too afraid to fail publicly, to write something less than perfect. But that's exactly the opposite of what we need to be doing. Adam Grant, author of *The Originals*, nails it: "You need a lot of bad ideas in order to get a few good ones. One of the best predictors of the greatness of a classical composer is the sheer number of compositions that they've generated. Bach, Beethoven, and Mozart had to generate hundreds and hundreds of compositions in order to get to a much smaller number of masterpieces. The starting point is that if most of us want to be more original, we have to generate more ideas."

So my plea to you is write more, and don't worry if every blog isn't *War and Peace*.

GIVE TIMELY FEEDBACK

Employees want to know:

>> What is expected of me?

>> How am I performing relative to these expectations?

>> What is my clear and simple path to promotion?

The best way to answer these questions is through regular, timely feedback. An entire book can be written on the best way to do that. For brevity's sake, I'll say that the best practice here involves regular one-on-one meetings between employee and manager (ideally for one hour every week), as well as performance reviews (ideally twice per year). I find Trello is a great tool to use for tracking one-on-ones. Throughout the week, you can add cards for topics you aim to discuss and you can also track action items with due dates. My go-to agenda for weekly meetings is:

>> What are the top three things you want to discuss?

>> What roadblocks are you facing with regard to (1) the strategic initiatives you are working on, (2) your day to day job, or (3) your SMART goals? (see below for details on SMART goals)

» What's working? What's not working?

» Action Items

AGENDA	TO DO THIS WEEK	IN-PROGRESS	DONE

For larger companies, one-on-ones are doable at scale. It really depends on how the team is structured and what the meeting rhythm of the team is. Some of the biggest companies in the world, including ESPN and Disney, hold one-on-one meetings in at least some pockets of the organization.

Pair one-on-ones with a 360-degree performance review twice a year. Most performance reviews are a waste of time. Yet it's possible to have useful, fair, productive performance reviews. Frank Dobbin and Alexandra Kalev discovered that while "90% of mid-size and large companies use annual performance ratings..., studies show that raters tend to lowball women and minorities in performance reviews." While it's vitally important to have a performance review process in place, an annual system with ratings clearly does nothing to help diversity and in fact hurts diversity initiatives.

Weekly one-on-ones are, in fact, performance reviews. They are timely check-ins and a great way to give and receive feedback. Focus on the areas where the employee went above and beyond as well as areas for improvement.

Performance reviews ought to include:

» **360-degree feedback:** Email 3–5 people who have diverse perspectives on the employee's performance. Ask each person you email to provide three strengths and three areas for improvement for the employee.

You do the same. Ask the employee to do the same for themselves. Go over all feedback with the employee.

» **SMART goals:** SMART goals are Specific, Measurable, Attainable, Realistic, Timely goals that the employee can work on achieving over the next six months. SMART goals should align with the skill categories the employee is developing to move up the career ladder. You should set clear expectations with the employee regarding the timeline to promotion. For example, if you do these three things, we expect you to be eligible for promotion in nine to twelve months. SMART goals should be reviewed in weekly one-on-ones.

SET UP MENTORSHIP PROGRAMS

Research has shown that the best way to enable individuals to have empathy for and become advocates of people who are not like them is to have them mentor individuals who are not like them. By creating a mentorship program inside your company, and encouraging employees to seek mentors outside of your organization, you are pairing individuals with each other in a way that's supportive. A mentor is an internal champion for their mentee. Mentees should be allowed to pick their own mentor, and even opt out of the mentor program. I'm not advocating any specific gendered pairings; I'm advocating an open and fluid mentorship program.

WHAT WORKS FOR HIRING?

Now that you've made your company as fair and inclusive an environment as you can, and you've committed to maintaining these good habits, you can finally turn to recruiting and hiring! Here are a few tips:

BECOME GENDER-NEUTRAL

The concept of gender-neutral job descriptions first became a talked-about thing around 2015. If you Google "gender-neutral job descriptions" you'll get a list of the latest thinking and advice on the topic. Current best practice is to use gender-neutral words in your job descriptions. As of the time of the writing of this book, the most useful tool I know of is Text.io (www.textio.com). Enter your job description and in two seconds you get it fully analyzed. Text.io will:

> » Highlight specific words that are masculine, feminine, cliché, and repeated too often.
> » Compare your job posting to hundreds of thousands of ones like it. My software engineering job was compared against 113,355 software engineering jobs recently analyzed in NYC.
> » Give you specific tips on how to improve.

GO BLIND

As recently as the 1970s, the top orchestras in the world had 5% women. Today, they have over 30% women. Yet the size of the orchestras, number of jobs, and population of applicants has remained stable. The reason for the dramatic increase in the percentage of women is the double-blind tryout. Orchestras realized they were being biased against women without realizing it. At first, they attempted to combat this unconscious bias by having candidates audition behind a curtain so that their music would be heard and their faces not seen. However, this didn't result in any change. Then, they started asking the candidates to remove their shoes before walking on stage behind the curtain. And voila—the percentage of women candidates jumped from 5% to 30%. Why? Even hearing the click of women's shoes was enough to give our brains a clue, which resulted in unconscious bias against women. Only by being fully blind to who was auditioning did the orchestras improve their gender balance.

Replicate this by having one step of your interview process be blind. My team asks candidates to submit a coding sample. Our recruiters share the code with our developers and hide the name of the candidate, so the graders do not know the identity of the person who wrote the code. Then developers give the code a grade of 1–5.

It is impossible for the entire interview process to be blind. Having one blind step in your process will make a big difference.

EMBRACE FALSE POSITIVES

A great way to test the non-blind areas of your interview process is to send through false positives. For example, let's say a recruiter phone screens a female developer and determines she's not qualified to proceed to the next step. Send her through to the next step anyway. Do this once in a while and see what you learn. You might learn you have hidden bias somewhere in your process, or you might learn you have a quality control issue. Or you might confirm that your vetting process is high-functioning.

If you feel like you are disrespecting the candidate's time by sending her through when you have already failed her, I encourage you to think again. If your process is indeed biased, then you've just given a woman a huge advantage by enabling her to make it through a step in the process she would have otherwise failed due to unconscious bias.

PRO TIP: WHEN PICKING WHICH FALSE POSITIVE TO SEND THROUGH, AVOID CHOOSING CANDIDATES WHO ARE AN OBVIOUS MISMATCH.
For example, if the job requires the employee to work onsite in

New York City, don't send through a candidate who is not able to work in New York City.

A NOTE ABOUT TARGETED RECRUITING AND HEADHUNTERS

Targeted recruiting. Is it legal? Is it fair? It can be both if done correctly.

There are two approaches you can take with targeted recruiting:

> » **Work with groups that represent women.** There are groups that represent women developers of all ages, including school ages. You can get as involved as you'd like: from hiring interns and apprentices, to sponsoring women to attend local conferences by paying for their tickets, to offering to tutor women in job interviewing, to hiring women at various levels. Some job boards that focus on women or people of color are People of Color in Tech, Women in Tech, or Women Who Code, HireTechLadies, FindMyFlock, Code2040.
> » **Target women.** Spend time getting to know women developers, and over time ask them if they'd like to work on your team. A great way to do this is to sponsor events. For example, you could have a Women Who Code breakfast once per quarter. You could offer free mentorship for women developers. Get creative here. There are many options for expanding your network of women in tech, or any other industry.

CASE STUDY: MEETUP

Yvette Pasqua, CTO at Meetup, believes that "while hiring junior women developers out of bootcamp is great, it will never get you to where you want to be. What other women want to see is women

HIRE WOMEN

in leadership roles. They want to see role models. They want to see people like them making decisions and running the company. If you put all your effort into hiring women into entry-level and mid-level roles, it's going to take you a really long time to get there and you might not get there because all those women may never see people above them and they opt out before they get there. Start by talking to and hiring as many women into leadership as you can. That's even more work that takes time and effort and you've got to be willing to put in the time."

Headhunters are tricky. Many are a waste of time, but I have had success with headhunters a handful of times. Headhunters can charge up to 20%–30% of the employee's base salary, so think about whether the money spent is worth it.

Use a headhunter if:
» You've exhausted all other options.
» The cost of delay (the amount of money we lose waiting to find the perfect candidate) is greater than the cost of the headhunter.
» You are seeking a specialized role and you have no one on your team who is able to vet candidates.

Don't use a headhunter if:
» The headhunter is going to do a search and wind up finding the same types of people you'd find on your own.

CONCLUSION

We've covered a lot of ground in a short amount of time. We've created the foundational core of equal pay and zero tolerance of harassment. On top of this, we've built an iterative process for discovering and removing bias in a prioritized, iterative way. And finally, we talked about a handful of tactical ways that we can work on removing bias in our hiring and retention processes.

As you tackle your biases one by one, remember that discovering and removing bias is a journey. Continuously learn from both your successes and your failures by holding retrospectives and measuring progress.

Hold retrospectives often. If you have a process for holding effective retrospectives that works for your software teams, mirror that process here. If you need help learning how to hold an effective retrospective, download the free ebook *How to Facilitate an Effective Retrospective* from Stride's website.

Every month, review progress towards your annual goal and measure progress. If your team has an agreed upon way of measuring progress for software projects, mirror it here. If you are seeking a process, I recommend setting 1–2 leading Key Performance Indicators (KPIs) and 1–2 lagging KPIs, and defining red/yellow/green for each. A leading KPI is something measurable that you believe will lead to your goal happening. A lagging KPI is a measure of past performance, and is in essence proof of your goal being achieved. Red/Yellow/Green tell us the definition of what bad, mediocre, and good look like, respectively. Here are some sample KPIs:

KPI	Red	Yellow	Green
% of phone screens/ month by gender (leading KPI)	<30%	30%–50%	>50%
% people falling out of interview at onsite stage by gender (leading KPI)	2 times as many women as men	1.5 times as many women as men	Equal percentages by gender
% of hires/month by gender (lagging KPI)	<30%	30%–50%	>50%

As you learn what works and what doesn't, iterate and embrace change. Revisit the hiring diagram in the Introduction often. Strike a healthy balance between execution and ideation, and keep making progress towards your goal.

CASE STUDY: AMY AND ERIC, PART 3

So how have Amy and Eric been faring in their quest to hire more women? They faced resistance several times, but they stuck with the process. Six months later, Amy and Eric reported back to the CEO that they had implemented weekly one-on-ones within the entire engineering team, written two blog posts on the company's commitment to diversity and inclusion, and created a quarterly Women Who Code breakfast. As a result, they hired two women and no women had left in the past six months!

Amy and Eric's passion for helping their company improve their diversity and inclusion efforts was strong, and their excitement was starting to spread to others. Their work wasn't done, yet they felt empowered and energized, and felt they were truly making a difference, one day at a time.

We all want to believe that every woman will get hired and retained based on her skills and achievement, based on merit. Yet this is simply naive. The truth of meritocracy is that, while individual achievement does play its part, societal realities play a bigger part. And so, unfortunately, we can't assume that women will one day get equal seats at the proverbial table because "they deserve it." Instead, we must all work together and proactively create inclusive hiring practices and work environments.

This being said, I realize that gender diversity is merely one small piece of a larger conversation around diversity and inclusion for all. Fortunately, the strategies shared throughout this book can serve as foundational practices that further diversity on a broader scale.

READING LIST

This book either cites directly or draws upon the following sources.

Anita Borg Institute. *The Case for Investing in Women* (March 2014). https://anitab.org/wp-content/uploads/2014/03/The-Case-for-Investing-in-Women-314.pdf

Bureau of Labor Statistics. *Comparison of U.S. and International Labor Turnover Statistics* (July 2015). https://www.bls.gov/opub/mlr/2015/article/comparison-of-u-s-and-international-labor-turnover-statistics-1.htm

Dobbin, Frank, and Alexandra Kalev. "Why Diversity Programs Fail." *Harvard Business Review* (July-August 2016). https://hbr.org/2016/07/why-diversity-programs-fail

Farnell, Richard. "Mentor People Who Aren't Like You." *Harvard Business Review* (April 17, 2017). https://hbr.org/2017/04/mentor-people-who-arent-like-you

Grant, Adam. *The Originals* (February 7, 2017).

Grant, Heidi, and David Rock. "Why Diverse Teams are Smarter." *Harvard Business Review* (November 4, 2016). https://hbr.org/2016/11/why-diverse-teams-are-smarter

Harvard Business Review blog series on diversity. https://hbr.org/topic/diversity

Hanlon, Jay. "Stack Overflow Isn't Very Welcoming. It's Time for That to Change." (April 26, 2018). https://stackoverflow.blog/2018/04/26/stack-overflow-isnt-very-welcoming-its-time-for-that-to-change/

Hubbard, Douglas. *How to Measure Anything: Finding the Value of Intangibles in Business* (March 17, 2014).

Hunt, Vivian. "Why Diversity Matters." McKinsey online (January 2015). https://www.mckinsey.com/business-functions /organization/our-insights/why-diversity-matters

Katsarou, Maria. *Women & the Leadership Labyrinth: Howard vs Heidi.* http://www.leadershippsychologyinstitute.com/women -the-leadership-labyrinth-howard-vs-heidi/

Madden, Debbie. "Binary Bias: Recoding Women's Place In Technology." *Huffington Post* (December 6, 2017). https://www .huffingtonpost.com/debbie-madden/binary-bias-recoding -womens-place-in-technology_b_7071406.html

Madden, Debbie. "What Uber's Future COO Must Do To Fix The Company." *CNBC* (March 9, 2017). https://www.cnbc.com/2017 /03/09/what-ubers-future-coo-must-do-to-fix-the-company -commentary.html

Mohr, Tara Sophia. "Why Women Don't Apply For Jobs Unless They're 100% Qualified". *Harvard Business Review* (August 25, 2014). https://hbr.org/2014/08/why-women-dont-apply-for-jobs-unless -theyre-100-qualified

Project Implicit (2011). https://implicit.harvard.edu/implicit /index.jsp

Reynolds, Alison, and David Lewis. "Teams Solve Problems Faster When They're More Cognitively Diverse." *Harvard Business Review*

(March 30, 2017). https://hbr.org/2017/03/teams-solve-problems
-faster-when-theyre-more-cognitively-diverse

The Robert Half 2018 Salary Guide. https://www.roberthalf.com
/salary-guide/technology

Robinson, Kristen. *A North Star for Diversity* (November 7, 2016).
http://blog.pandora.com/pandora-news/a-north-star-for-diversity/

Sinek, Simon. *Start With Why: How Great Leaders Inspire Everyone
to Take Action* (2009).

ACKNOWLEDGMENTS

September 5, 2015 changed my life forever. I discovered what I'd soon learn was a 6.2cm tumor. At age 40, I was diagnosed with aggressive Stage II breast cancer. The next year was one for the record books. I was running Stride Consulting, going through treatment, and trying to be there for my husband Rex and our two kids Brooke and Dylan. By the time summer of 2016 rolled around, I was cured. And exhausted. Over the next two years, I focused on healing.

And then it happened. I woke up one day and didn't think about cancer. And then weeks went by when I didn't think about it. And then months.

People often ask "What was it like?" The better question is "What IS it like?" Having cancer changed my perspective on things. On everything. And it always will. The single best thing to come out of having cancer is that when I feel like doing a thing, no matter how scared I am to try it, I do it.

So, when I caught up with Josh back in 2017 and he asked what I was up to I said, "I'd love to write a book one day." And he said, "Vicky, Jeff, and I just happen to run a press company. We'd love to help you write that book."

And so it was.

I can't thank Josh Seiden, Jeff Gothelf, and Vicky Olsen at Sense & Respond Press enough. They were true partners in the effort to get this book written and I truly could not have done it without them.

The Stride Consulting team. For those who joined in 2014 and early 2015, when I called you up and I said, "we've got no funding, we've got no clients. But, we have a great idea and it's going to be great. I give you my word that I'll always care and that I'll always do right by you." And you said "I'm in." Thank you. For those who joined in 2015 and 2016, while I was battling cancer and I said, "I'm going through a thing but don't worry, it'll all be ok." And you said "I'm in." Thank you. And for those who joined in 2017 and 2018 and I said, "we're growing now, and we don't yet have it all figured out, but what we do have is the best group of people I've ever worked with, and a culture that's second to none, and all I ask is that you speak honestly and tell me when you think I'm making a mistake." And you said "I'm in." Thank you.

Brooke and Dylan. You are my sunshine. You make me proud every single day and I am lucky to be your mom.

Rex. You are my rock. From the moment we met in 1995 you have been my partner in crime. I only hope that through the years I have done all I can to deserve your love.

DEBBIE MADDEN is the founder and CEO of Stride Consulting, an Agile software development consultancy that helps enterprise, midmarket, and startup tech teams like *The New York Times*, Saks Fifth Avenue, Sony, and Major League Baseball become the highest-functioning versions of themselves. By coding alongside teams and providing technical mentorship, Striders help clients build efficient software, and give the entire team a true competitive advantage in perpetuity. Debbie is a serial entrepreneur, mother, wife, writer, speaker, and breast cancer survivor. She has built five companies from the ground up, and has been CEO of two Inc 500 companies. Debbie has written for *Inc.com*, *Harvard Business Review*, CNBC, *The Huffington Post*, *Forbes*, *Forbes Women*, *Computer World*, InfoQ and more.

www.stridenyc.com

debbiemadden1

Made in the USA
Middletown, DE
15 January 2020